GO FACTS TRANSPORT
On the Road

On the Road

© Blake Publishing 2003
Additional material © A & C Black Publishers Ltd 2005

First published 2003 in Australia by Blake Education Pty Ltd

This edition published 2005 in the United Kingdom by
A & C Black Publishers Ltd, 37 Soho Square, London W1D 3QZ
www.acblack.com

Published by permission of Blake Publishing Pty Ltd, Glebe NSW, Australia.

ISBN-10: 0-7136-7284-6
ISBN-13: 978-0-7136-7284-8

A CIP record for this book is available from the British Library.

Written by Ian Rohr
Design and layout by The Modern Art Production Group
Photos by Laura North, Photodisc, Corel, Corbis, Photo Alto, Photo Spin,
Image Ideas, Comstock, Eyewire and Ingram.

UK series consultant: Julie Garnett

Printed in China by WKT Company Ltd.

A & C Black uses paper produced with elemental chlorine-free pulp,
harvested from managed sustainable forests.

Contents

Sharing the Road

Cars, trucks, motorcycles and bicycles all share the road.

People use roads to get to places. You might take a bus to school or ride a bicycle to the park.

Cyclist

Some people drive cars or ride motorcycles to work. **Pedestrians** walk along pavements and cross roads on crossings.

Some people work as drivers. Bus and taxi drivers take people to different places. Some truck drivers drive their loads long distances.

motorcycle

truck

car

Rules of the Road

Rules help keep people safe when they share the road.

All drivers need to know the rules of the road. Drivers of **vehicles** like cars, motorcycles or trucks must pass a test before they can drive. Drivers must be careful because traffic accidents can be very dangerous.

Stop sign

Traffic signs give drivers important information. Some signs tell drivers the speed limit. The speed limit is the fastest speed allowed. Other signs tell drivers to watch out for animals on the road or for pedestrian crossings.

This sign warns drivers that deer may be on the road.

This sign tells drivers to slow down for children.

Cars should stop at crossings when people are waiting to cross.

Cars

There are more cars on the road than any other vehicle.

Cars are made in many shapes and sizes. On any road you might see family cars, vans, taxis and sports cars.

Some cars, such as racing cars and sports cars, are built to be very fast. Family cars are built for safety. They are heavier than sports cars.

Most cars run on petrol but some modern cars can use electricity, **solar energy** or natural gas.

Buying petrol

Racing cars compete on race tracks.

Electric Powered

This car is powered by electricity.

DID YOU KNOW?
50 million cars are made each year. There are over 500 million cars in the world.

It takes about 20 000 different parts to make a car.

Buses and Taxis

People pay money to use buses and taxis.

Buses usually follow the same **route** every day. Bus drivers pick up people at bus stops. School buses take children to and from school. Children don't pay **fares** on school buses.

People pay fares to go to places in taxis. People often use taxis to get to and from airports. In a big city, taxi drivers drive to thousands of different places.

Bus

This bus takes people to all the interesting places in London.

Some modern buses have wheelchair lifts.

Black taxi cabs are common in London.

11

Trucks

People use trucks to move goods and do other work.

Trucks come in different shapes and sizes and do different kinds of work. Trucks carry many different kinds of goods such as furniture, computers or food. Food trucks are often refrigerated.

Trucks with long **trailers** can carry large loads, such as cars and logs. The front part of the truck has the engine and driver's cab or seat. The back part is a trailer that carries the load.

18-wheeler

Trucks often travel the long distances between cities.

Trucks can carry heavy loads, such as logs.

BIGGEST!
Trucks are the biggest vehicles on the road. They can weigh as much as 50 cars.

Long trucks, called road trains, are used in the Australian outback.

13

Travel by Night

In some countries truck drivers can choose to travel at night when the roads are not so busy.

It is dangerous to drive for a long time without resting so many truck drivers travel the long distances between cities at night and rest during the day. Trucks often have beds behind the front seat where the driver can sleep.

Petrol station

Truck drivers can eat, rest and get fuel at restaurants and petrol stations along their routes. Some of these are open all night.

This petrol station is open 24 hours a day.

In Australia truck drivers on long trips sometimes travel together for safety.

 Glossary

fare   the price to ride in a vehicle like a bus or taxi

pedestrian   a person going somewhere by walking

route   a path that is travelled, such as the way a bus travels each day

solar energy   energy from the sun

traffic   the vehicles and pedestrians on a route

trailer   a vehicle built to be pulled by another vehicle

vehicle   a car, bus or other thing that carries people or goods

 Index